MY LONG COVID VACATION

Written by: Ella Dembeck
Illustrated by: Lizette Duvenage

One day Samantha woke up and was told that her school was closed, because of a virus that made people sick.

"No school"? thought Sam" Hooray! No more math", which she hated because she was not good with numbers. No more Kevin, who keeps telling her that he was faster than her, smarter than her, and even bigger than her, though only by 2 inches.

The first few days she enjoyed sleeping in, playing with her favourite toys, and playing games on her tablet.

But then she started to get
bored and she missed her friends and even
school.

She felt sad and asked her mom when she could go back to school. Her mom explained to her that the virus had become a pandemic, which means it spread to a large number of people around the world, making them sick.

Sam worried that her family might get sick, but her mom wrapped her arms around her and told her that staying home will protect everyone.

Staying home and not being able to play with your friends can be lonely and sad.

To deal with her sadness, mom suggested Samantha write about her feelings in a daily notebook she called a journal.

Sam started writing in her journal. Writing about her feelings made her feel better and soon enough she was writing about other things that came to her mind like: how are her friends doing during the pandemic? Or what does the virus look like?

She started thinking of all the people who got sick because of the virus and all the doctors and nurses, who work in hospitals every day to help sick people.

One day she decided to make a big poster for all the frontline workers. She wrote "Thank You!" in big letters and drew little red hearts all around the edges with one big heart right under the words:

"Thank You"!

She wanted to talk to her best friend Chloe and mom suggested that she video chat with her. That way they could talk and see each other. Mom helped her set up a Skype chat and soon enough she saw Chloe's face on her computer screen in front of her.

As they chatted and laughed with each other, Sam started to feel happy again. Talking to her friend Chloe really helped.

During one of her video chats, Chloe played a song for her that she learned on the piano. This made Sam interested in music and she picked up her dad's guitar. With his help she learned to play some simple notes. It was hard at first, but soon enough Sam learned to play some easy songs.

She also helped her mom with cooking and baking, and her mom helped Sam with some schoolwork. Sam loved spending more time with her family.

One day her mom told her that the virus was infecting less people because everyone stayed home, and that small groups of people were allowed to be together.

Her family and Chloe's family became a cohort, meaning a small group of people hanging out together. Sam and Chloe could finally have real playdates together.

One sunny afternoon, Chloe brought some big cardboard boxes over to build a castle. They built a big castle in Sam's backyard. They used scissors, tape and paint.

When they were done, they brought out blankets and pillows and cookies that Sam made with her mom the day before, and they had a royal picnic just outside the castle.

The next playdate Sam went to Chloe's house. They played a pretend game where only the girls could defeat the virus with their magic powers.

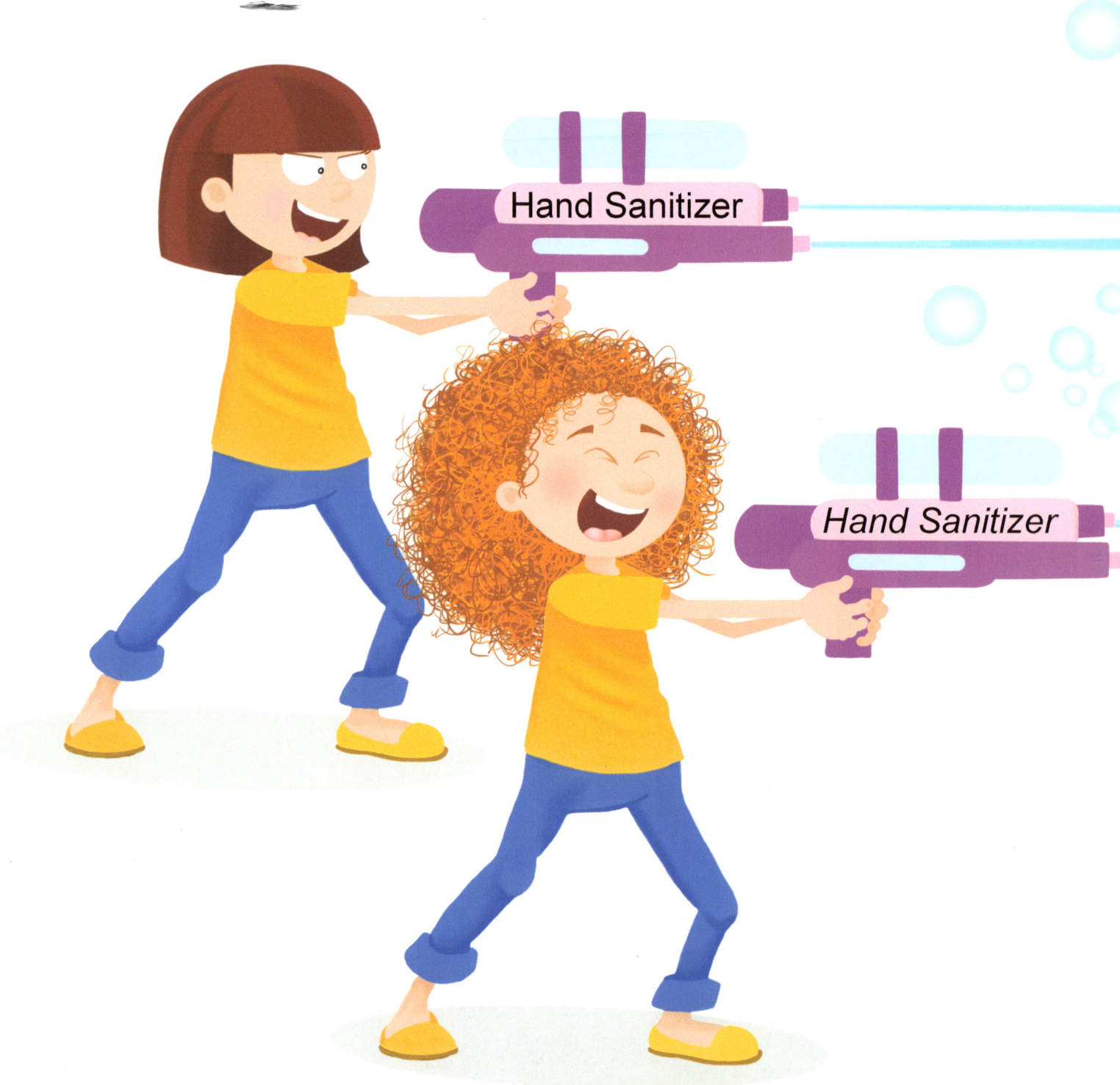

Even Kevin was so impressed and called her a hero!

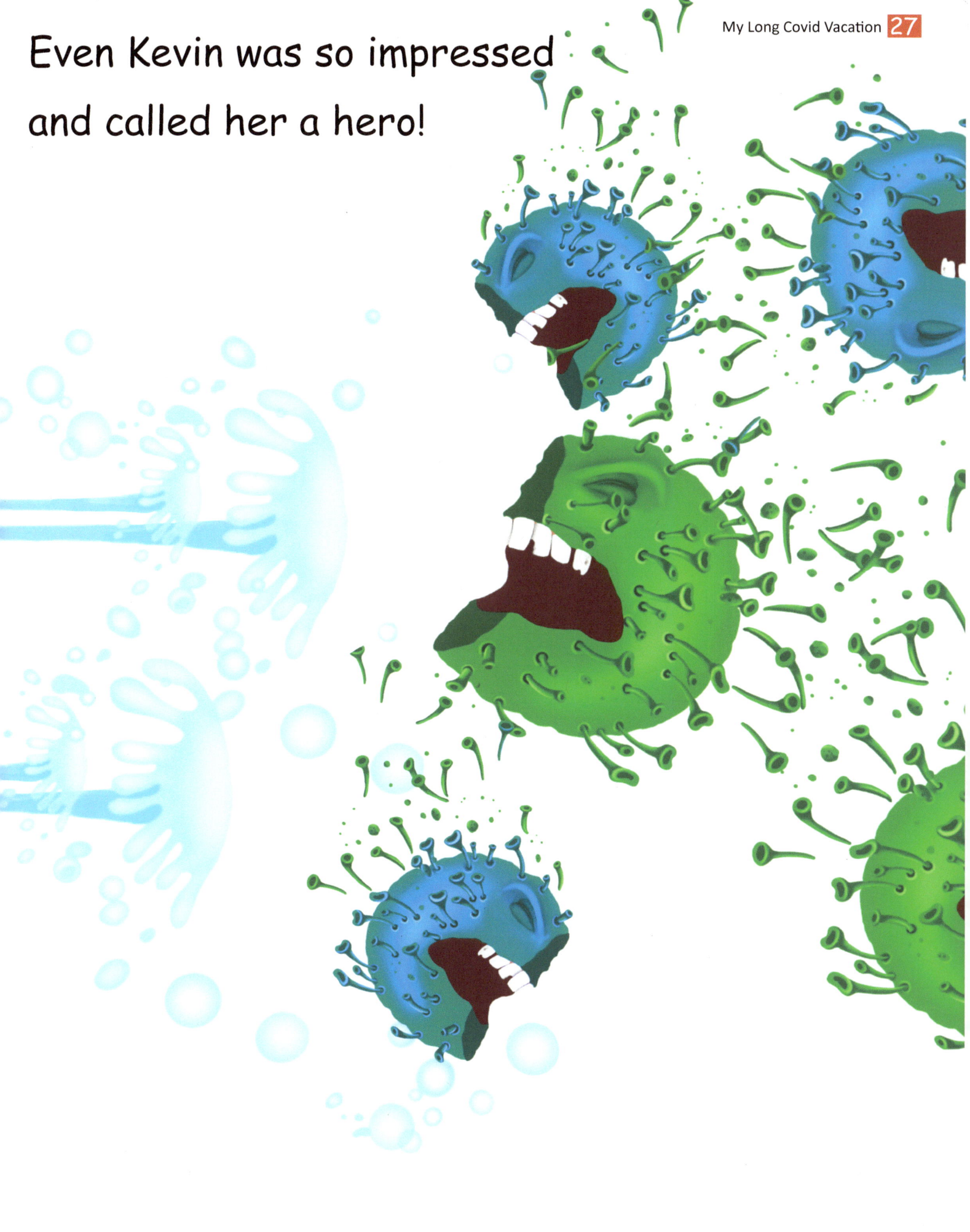

6 Feet Apart

6 Feet Apart

Sam's mom said that they could go outside the house for walks now, as long as they practice social distancing.

Social distancing means staying 6 feet apart. She asked her Mom why?

She said that the virus spreads from one person to another and when we keep our distance from others, we help each other stay safe.

They also had to wear face masks. Sam's face mask was green with yellow flowers on it. Chloe's was pink with red ladybugs.

Sam asked her mom when she can go back to school to see all of her friends again.

She said:" I know it's frustrating. We don't know, but it won't last forever. And if we all do our part, it will be soon enough to make things better.

So, Sam makes sure she follows all the steps to prevent the spread:

1) Practice social distancing. Stay 6 feet apart
2) Wear a face mask to prevent others from getting sick
3) Sneeze and cough into your elbows
4) Wash your hands a lot with soap and water
5) Try not to touch your face.

We count on you to do the same.

Remember: We are all in this together!

My Long Covid Vacation

The year 2020 has been a scary and confusing year, but you are not alone. Many children around the world felt the same as you and like Samantha in this story.
Let's talk about your experience during lock down:

How did you feel when you first heard that schools are closed, and you had to stay home? Where you happy like Samantha?

_____
_____
_____

How did you feel after four weeks of staying home and not be able to see your friends? Samantha was lonely and missed her friends.

_____
_____
_____

What did you learn about the corona virus?

_____
_____
_____

Samantha wrote in her diary to help with her sadness. What helped you deal with your sadness?

_____
_____
_____
_____

Samantha learned how to play the guitar. What new skills or hobbies did you learn during lock down?

_____
_____
_____

Ingram Content Group UK Ltd.
Milton Keynes UK
UKHW051909260423
420851UK00002B/38